The BOYS' book of THINGS TO MAKE

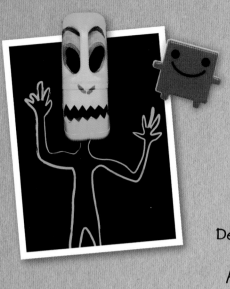

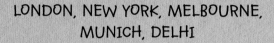

LONDON, NEW YORK, MELBOURNE,
MUNICH, DELHI

Editor James Mitchem
Senior Designer Sadie Thomas
Designers Charlotte Bull, Ria Holland, Poppy Joslin
Photography Andy Crawford
Additional editing Grace Redhead, Nikki Sims
Managing Editor Penny Smith
Managing Art Editor Marianne Markham
Category Publisher Mary Ling
Art Director Jane Bull
Pre-Production Producer Rebecca Fallowfield
Senior Producer Charlotte Oliver
Jacket Designer Wendy Bartlet
Special Sales Creative Project Manager Alison Donovan

This edition published in 2014
First published in Great Britain in 2013 by
Dorling Kindersley Limited, 80 Strand, London WC2R 0RL

A Penguin Random House Company

3 5 7 9 8 6 4 2
002–187173–Jun/14

A CIP catalogue record for this book is available
from the British Library

ISBN: 978-1-4093-4803-0

Printed and bound in China
by South China Printing Co. Ltd.

Discover more at www.dk.com

The BOYS' book of THINGS TO MAKE

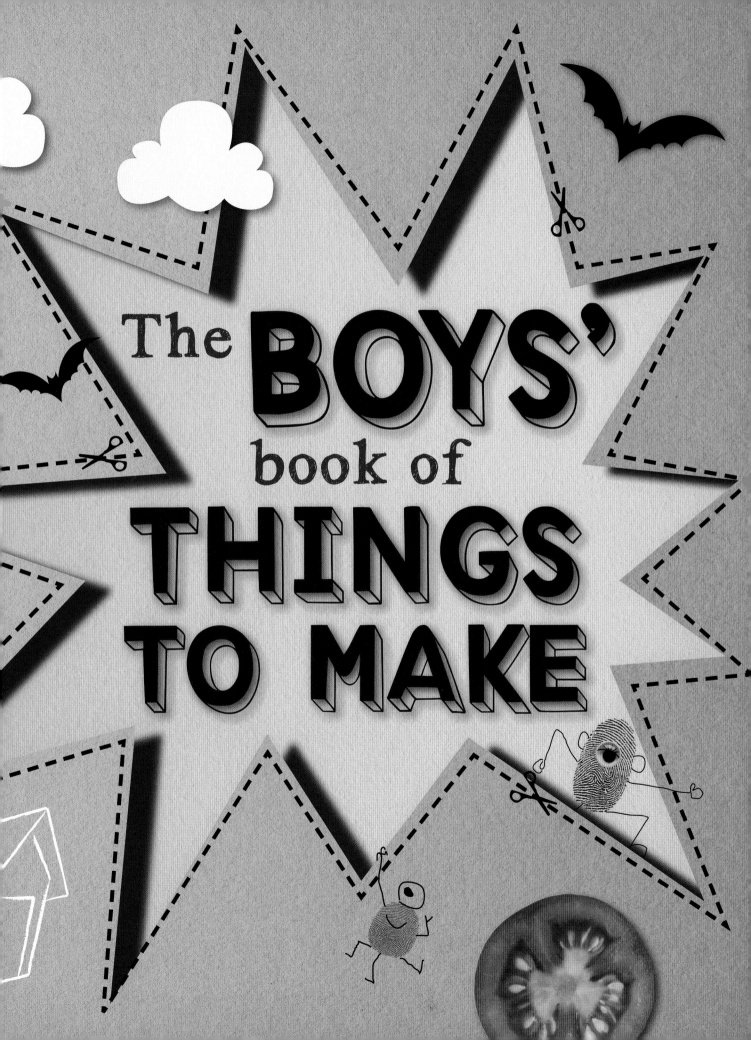

Contents

Milk planets

Come on, join the fun!

Knight puppet

Soap monsters

Urban periscope

Submarines use periscopes to stay out of sight while checking out what's on the surface. You too can **PEEK OVER WALLS** and **AROUND CORNERS** without being seen using this handheld version. Perfect for budding secret agents!

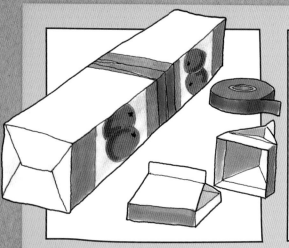

1 Cut the tops off the juice cartons. Clean the cartons, then tape them together in the middle to form one long tube.

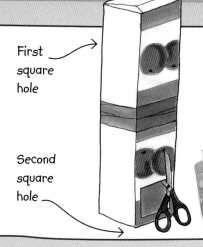

First square hole

Second square hole

2 Cut a square hole near the bottom of the tube, then turn the tube upside down and cut another hole on the opposite side.

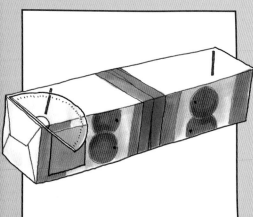

3 Put the tube on its side and use a protractor to mark a 45° angle sloping away from the square holes.

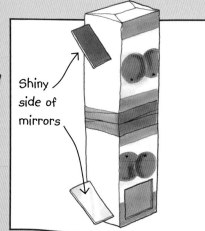

Shiny side of mirrors

4 Cut out slits along the marks the same length as the mirrors. Slide in the mirrors so the shiny sides face each other, as shown.

HOW IT WORKS
Mirrors reflect almost all of the light that falls on them, and they only reflect it in one direction. The periscope reflects the light from one mirror to the other, and then into our eyes so we see the image.

Light enters the periscope here

The light is reflected from this mirror

Look through here

This second mirror reflects the light into your eyes

Balloon drag racer

Make your own balloon-powered drag racing car using things you might find lying around the house. Why not **ORGANIZE A RACE** and ask your friends to build cars too? Who will be the winner?

You will need

- Straw
- Sticky tape
- Plastic bottle
- Wooden skewers
- Cardboard
- Scissors
- Blu-tack
- Plastic tubing
- Balloon
- Rubber band

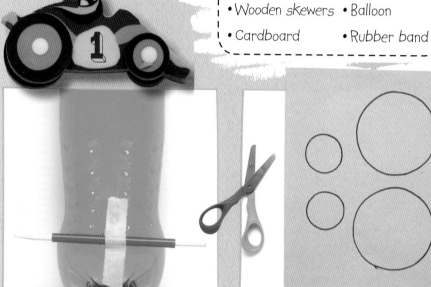

Make sure the straws are level

1 Cut the straw in half. Then firmly tape the two halves to the same side of the top and bottom of the plastic bottle.

2 Put the skewers through the straws. They need to be loose enough so that they can turn without getting stuck.

3 Draw around something circular on the cardboard for two large and two small wheels. Cut these out.

The tubing should be about 12cm (5in) long

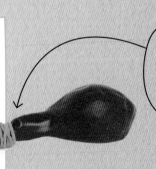

Make sure the rubber band doesn't cut off the air supply

4 Mark a dot in the middle of the wheels and poke the skewers through. Secure each wheel in place with the Blu-tack.

5 Insert the plastic tubing into the balloon and wrap the rubber band around it to keep it in place.

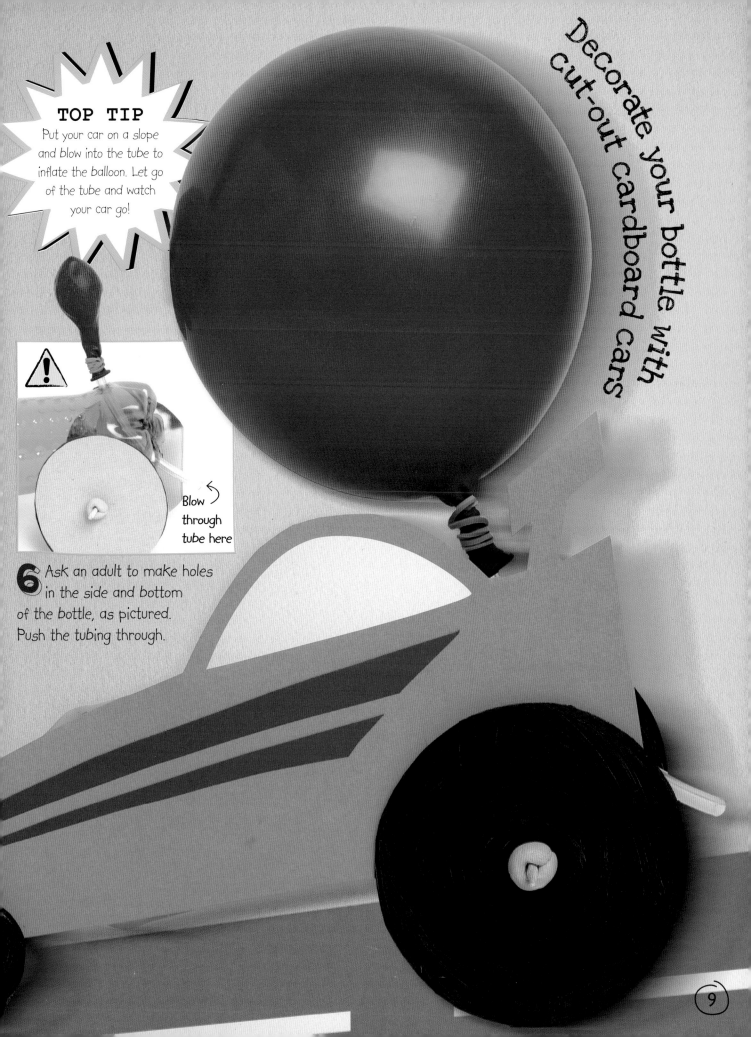

TOP TIP

Put your car on a slope and blow into the tube to inflate the balloon. Let go of the tube and watch your car go!

Blow through tube here

6 Ask an adult to make holes in the side and bottom of the bottle, as pictured. Push the tubing through.

Paper planes

You don't need a fancy kit or special glue to make a **COOL AEROPLANE**. Just learn the right sequence of folds to build **YOUR OWN FLYING MACHINE** – anytime, anywhere.

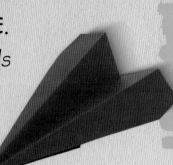

You will need

- Sheets of paper
- Paints
- Pens
- Stickers

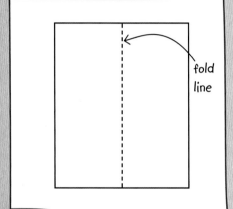

fold line

1 Fold the paper in half lengthways, then unfold it to create a line along the middle.

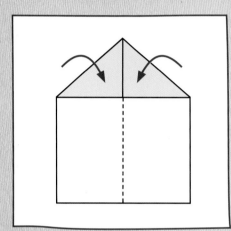

2 Fold two corners over towards the line to create a pointed top. Make sure they are the same size.

If the nose gets crumpled in a crash, the plane won't fly properly. You can protect the nose by folding it back on itself

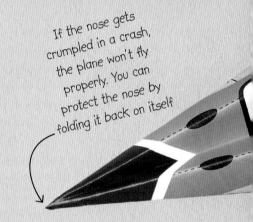

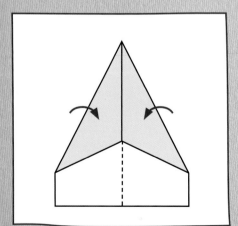

3 Neatly fold the sides in towards the middle. Flatten and smooth out all the folds.

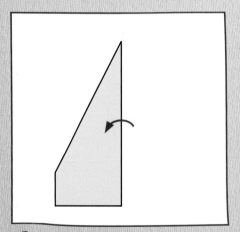

4 Fold one side of the plane across the middle and lay the plane out flat.

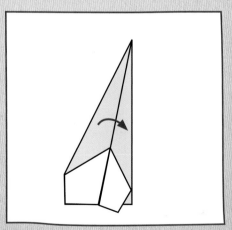

5 Fold one of the diagonal edges back along the straight side. Then repeat for the other side.

Crisp folds make the plane stiffer, which helps the plane to keep its shape

Fighter jet

Now, find some space and launch your plane!

If you lift one of the flaps slightly, your plane will fly in a spiral

Rocket

IN YOUR HANGAR

You can make your own squadron of planes and design how they look. Try different coloured paper, and add details and symbols with paint and stickers.

EXPERIMENT

Why not see if you can come up with other ways of making planes?

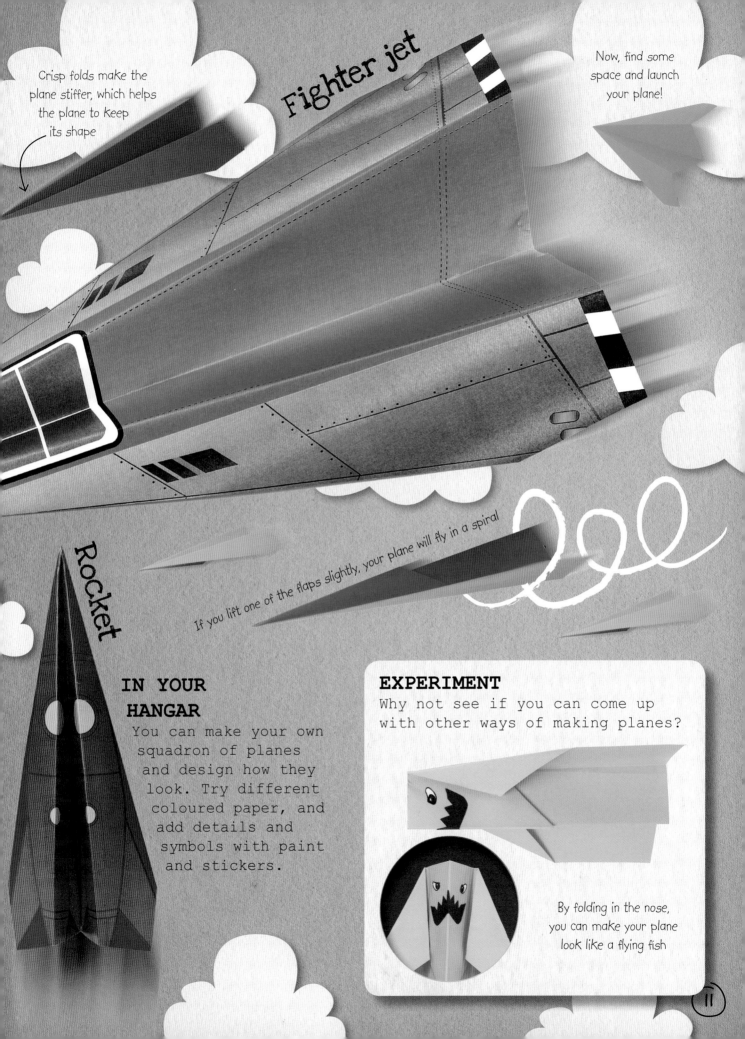

By folding in the nose, you can make your plane look like a flying fish

Recycled robots

Set your own **SCRAPHEAP CHALLENGE** and build a robot from junk or the recycling box. What **KINDS OF CHARACTERS** will you create?

1 Collect your materials and sketch out a design for your robots. Or just use this sketch of a robot head.

2 Attach the door stop to the sink drainer with glue, and then stick it to the tin can and leave it to dry.

3 Glue magnets to the can where you want the eyes, nose, and mouth, then attach bolts and screws.

Door stop

Sink drainer

Magnet

Bolt

Magnet

Circular items work well as eyes

Robot gallery

You can make robot characters out of almost anything: screws, brushes, tins, cutlery, hooks, bolts – whatever you can find! Just look for interesting parts and be creative.

Old forks make good feet!

Alien masks

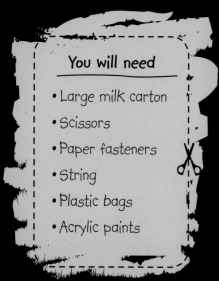

Whether you want a **FUNKY WALL DECORATION** for your room or the start of a scary **HALLOWEEN OUTFIT**, these alien masks fit every bill. So, now to the task of sourcing the cartons. Glass of milk, anyone?

You will need

- Large milk carton
- Scissors
- Paper fasteners
- String
- Plastic bags
- Acrylic paints

If you're making the masks as decorations, use a variety of different sized cartons

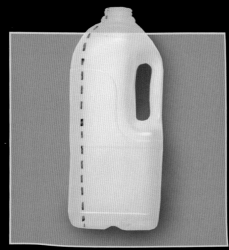

1 Mark a dotted line all the way around the front of the milk carton. Cut off the front side.

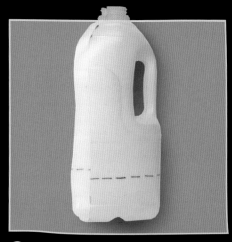

2 Next mark a line across the carton as shown above. Cut it off to make a detachable jaw.

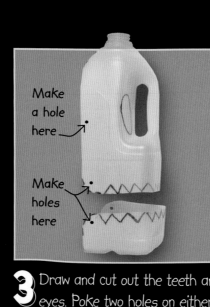

Make a hole here

Make holes here

3 Draw and cut out the teeth and eyes. Poke two holes on either side where the head and jaw will meet, and two more behind the eyes.

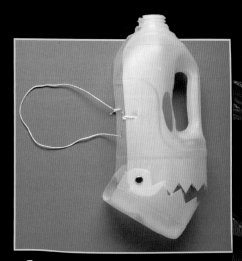

4 Insert the paper fasteners through the holes to attach the jaw and head, and poke string through the holes behind the eyes.

TOP TIP
Use different coloured strips of plastic bags to create crazy hair or stringy beards.

TOP TIP
Use glow-in-the-dark paint to make these masks even scarier!

15

Secret book safe

The best hiding places are the least obvious. And what could be more **ORDINARY** than a book on a shelf? But even though this book is right under anyone's nose, it has a secret...

You will need

- Glue
- Water
- Old book
- Brush
- Ruler
- Craft knife

1 Dilute the glue with a little water. Open the book and, leaving a few pages untouched at the front, brush the sides with the glue.

Once dry, brush with glue again

2 Close the book and use some post it notes to separate the pages you saved. Weigh it down with another book until the glue dries.

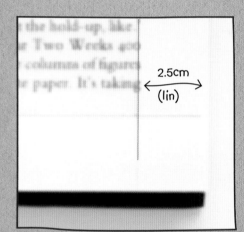

2.5cm (1in)

3 Open the book and fold back the saved pages. Using a ruler, draw a rectangle about 2.5cm (1in) from the edges on the next page.

4 Ask an adult to cut out the rectangle with a craft knife. It's dangerous, so don't try to do this yourself.

Make all the pages stick together

5 Brush the insides of the book with the glue and leave it to dry. You might need to do this a few times to get it to stick properly.

6 To neaten the cut edges, stick one of the spare pages over the top and trim just in from the sides.

Fill your book with
what you want to
hide and put it
back on the shelf

Glue two lolly sticks together to make a sword

Tape it in place to stop it slipping down the string

5 Cut two paper cups and kitchen roll tubes down to the right size for the arms and head. Thread the kitchen roll tubes and the cups, bases first, onto the arm strings.

If you want to give your Knight personality try adding eyes

6 To make the head, make holes in the centre of the bases of two paper cups. Cut one cup and place it over the other. Thread the leg strings through the head and tie the strings to a stick.

7 Paint the Knight silver, and cut a shield and breastplate out of cardboard. Cover them with felt and attach to the puppet.

Loop the arm string through the back of the shield and tie it to the stick at the top

Knight puppet

Recycle your rubbish to bring a Knight **TO LIFE**. Now, what to call him? Sir Plus, perhaps?

Start here

1 Take a long piece of string. Tie a knot at one end and a safety pin to the other. Make a hole in the bottom of a cup and thread the end with the safety pin through from inside. Tape the knot to the inside of the cup.

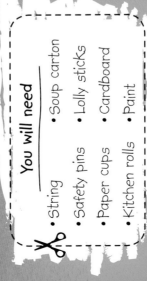

2 Cut a kitchen roll tube in half and thread the string up through it. Repeat step 1 to make the second leg.

3 Make two holes in the bottom of a soup carton and thread the string of each leg through.

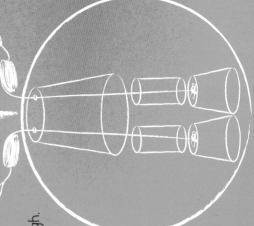

4 Make a hole in either side of the soup carton. Tie knots in two new pieces of string and thread through each hole.

Musical instruments

You will need

- Balloons
- Tin cans
- Rubber bands

Feeling like making some noise? Well, there's no need for expensive keyboards, guitars, or drum kits to **BANG OUT A TUNE**. Just lay your hands on some jars, tin cans, and the all-important spoon.

Jar xylophone

You will need

- Empty jars
- Spoon
- Water
- Food colouring

Add water to some jars and you'll have a range of dings to play a tune. More water creates a deeper sound; less water makes it sound higher. Use different food colourings to keep track of which sounds are which.

Handheld bongos

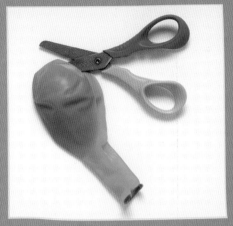

1 Cut along the edge of a balloon so that you end up with a big, flat piece of rubbery material.

2 Stretch the balloon over the rim of a tin can and secure it very tightly with elastic bands.

3 Add and secure a second balloon. Cut tiny holes in the top balloon for decoration.

Beat out a rhythm!

TOP TIP
Use different-sized tins to produce a range of sounds on your homemade drum kit.

Glow-in-the-dark jelly

Take jelly to a whole new level by using **A SPECIAL INGREDIENT** – tonic water – to make it glow under UV light. Perfect for a Halloween party.

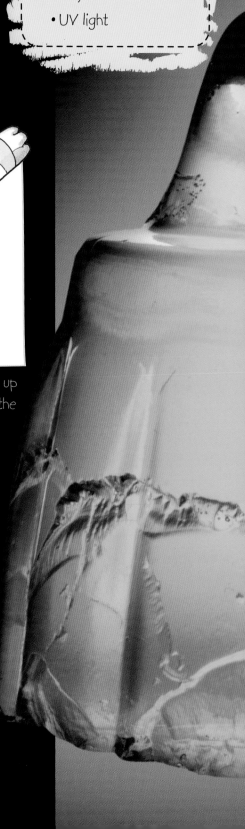

1 Follow the instructions on the jelly packet, but use tonic water instead of regular water.

2 If the instructions say to, top up the jelly. Add sugar to make the jelly taste less bitter.

3 Pour the mixture into a jelly mould or bowl and put it in the refrigerator to set.

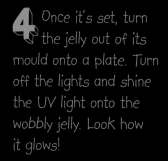

4 Once it's set, turn the jelly out of its mould onto a plate. Turn off the lights and shine the UV light onto the wobbly jelly. Look how it glows!

Tonic water contains a substance called QUININE, which causes the jelly to glow

TOP TIP
Inexpensive UV lights can be found in most hardware shops or on the Internet.

Erupting volcano

Be an amateur vulcanologist from the safety of your own kitchen. Make this smaller-than-normal **TABLE-TOP VOLCANO** and watch the **LAVA** erupt from its summit.

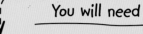

1 Fill the bottle about three-quarters full with warm water. Add the baking soda and mix together until dissolved.

2 Add a few drops of red food colouring, pop the lid on, and shake until mixed. Then add a drop of washing-up liquid.

3 Pile damp sand around the bottle to make it look like a volcano. If you prefer, you can use papier mâché instead.

4 Pour vinegar into your volcano. Sit back and watch the red lava flow!

REAL VOLCANOES don't work the same way. Your volcano erupts because the baking soda and vinegar cause a reaction when they're mixed. A real volcano erupts when molten rock (magma) forces its way up from the ground under massive pressure.

Argh, run away!

Soap monsters

You will need

- Bars of soap
- Plate
- Microwave
- Paperclips, googly eyes, pipe cleaners, and ring pulls

Did you know that your microwave can *be* **A MONSTER FACTORY?** Follow these instructions to create your own family of crazy monsters.

Once the monsters are fully cooled, decorate them in funny ways

Take a bar of soap and put it on a plate. Ask an adult to microwave it on the highest setting for two minutes. Let it cool down *before* taking it out of the microwave, as it will be very hot.

Meet my family

HOW IT WORKS
The heat from the microwave causes water molecules in the soap to form bubbles, which expand, causing the bars of soap to grow.

My brother Max

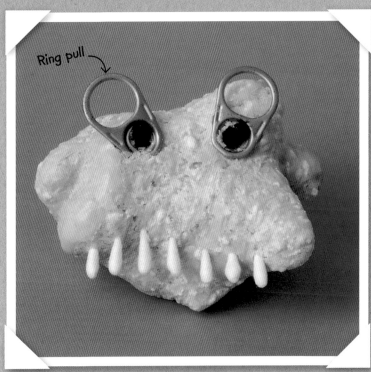

Ring pull

Dad

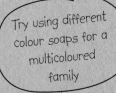

Try using different colour soaps for a multicoloured family

My brother Norman

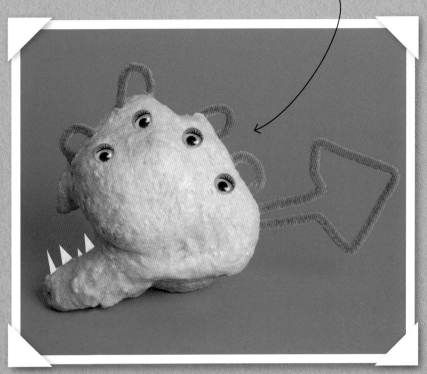

Mum

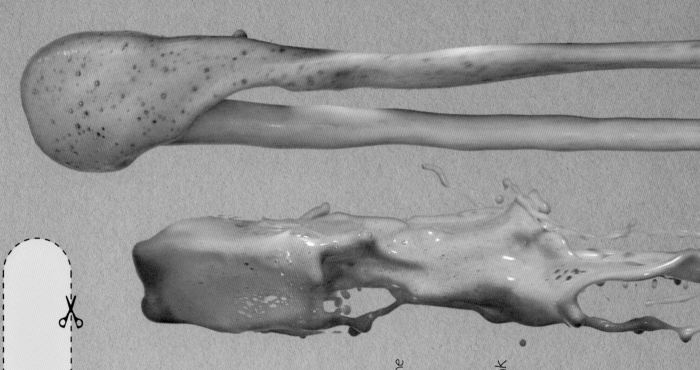

Soda fountain

What happens when you mix a mint with a fizzy drink? Something **VERY VERY MESSY**. After trying this experiment, you'll never want to eat them at the same time again!

1 Roll up a piece of card. Put the card in the neck of a bottle of fizzy drink.

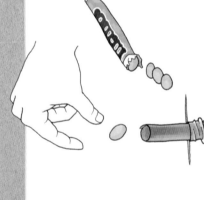

2 Push a toothpick through the card so it rests on the rim of the bottle. Drop a few mints on top.

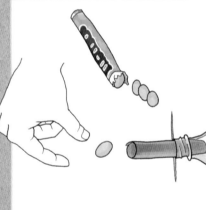

3 When you're ready, pull out the toothpick so the mints fall into the bottle. Quickly pull out the cardboard tube, stand back and watch the drink shoot into the air!

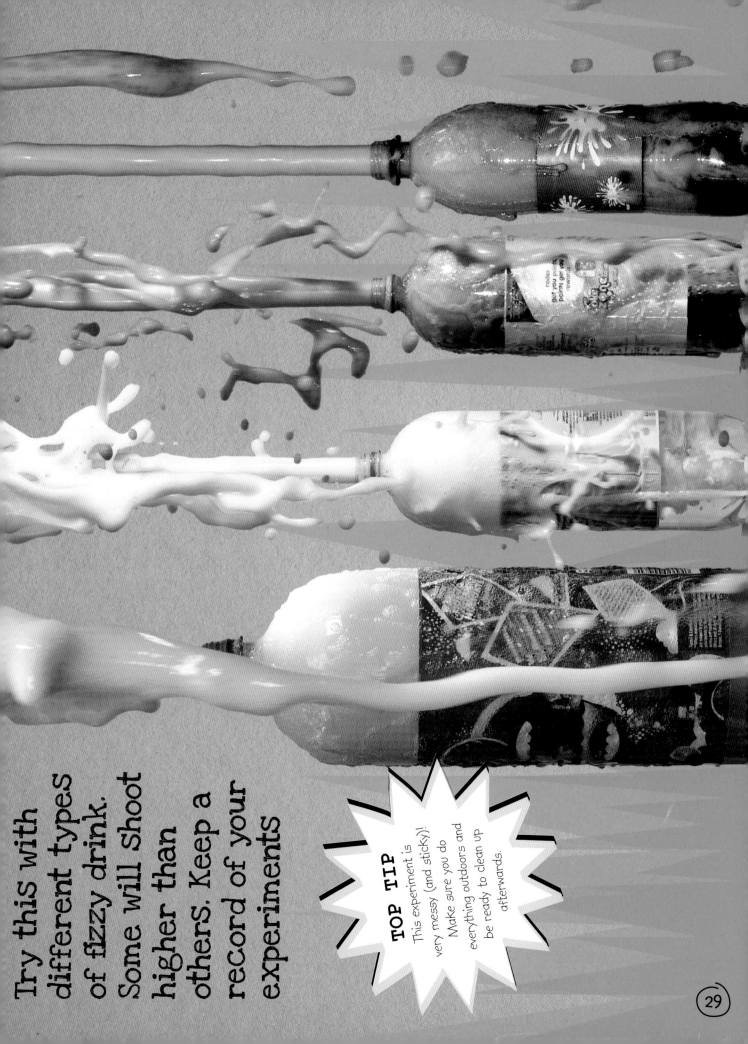

Try this with different types of fizzy drink. Some will shoot higher than others. Keep a record of your experiments

TOP TIP
This experiment is very messy (and sticky)! Make sure you do everything outdoors and be ready to clean up afterwards.

Make your own slime

IS SLIME A SOLID OR A LIQUID? It's actually both. Strictly it's a non-Newtonian fluid, which means that although it's a liquid, it can behave like a solid. Make a batch and see for yourself.

1 Fill a mug with cornflour and pour it into a mixing bowl.

2 Add half a glass of water and stir it all together.

3 Add a few drops of food colouring and mix together.

What can you do with your slime?

Try stretching it out or rolling it into a ball

How does it feel?

When you've made your slime, pick it up and see how it feels. If you squeeze the mixture it should feel solid, but if you hold it loosely it will flow, more like a liquid.

Mmmm slime!

Use different food colourings to change the appearance of your slime

Come on in, it's lovely

Launch a bottle rocket

While your back garden might not rival NASA's Cape Canaveral for **ROCKET LIFT-OFF**, you can use a similar scientific principle to launch a bottle-sized rocket of your own.

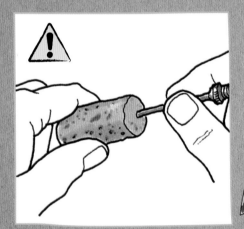

1 Push the needle adaptor from the pump all the way through the cork. You will probably need an adult to help you.

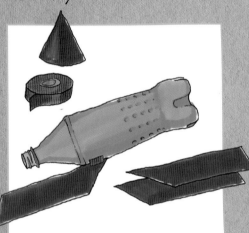

2 Cut four fins for your rocket from the card. Turn the bottle upside down and tape the fins on so they stand up, making sure to leave enough room underneath for the pump.

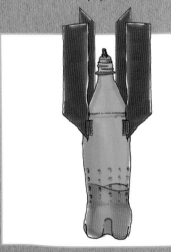

3 Fill the bottle one-quarter full with water. Push the cork in. It should be a really tight fit. If it isn't, take it out and wrap tape around it.

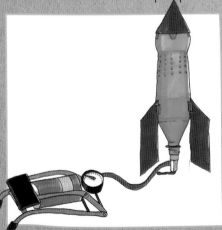

4 Stand the bottle up and attach the pump to the needle. Place the bottle as far away from the pump as possible.

5 Get everybody to stand well back and get an adult to start pumping, so you'll have the best view for lift-off.

HOW IT WORKS

When you pump air into the bottle (you'll see the bubbles in the water), it increases the air pressure inside the bottle. Once the air pressure inside becomes high enough, it forces out the cork, releasing the water and launching the bottle rocket high into the air.

Pinhole camera

A camera obscura (darkened room) is a box that projects an **UPSIDE-DOWN IMAGE** of the object in front of it, through a tiny pinhole. It's an ancient device, but it led to the invention of the **CAMERA**! Here's how to make one.

I'm ready for my close up!

TOP TIP
Your subject needs to be well lit to produce a sharp image. Try pointing your camera at something outdoors, or near a window.

You will need

- Empty cube-shaped tissue box
- Kitchen roll tube
- Coloured tissue paper
- Magnifying glass
- Tape
- Tracing paper

1 Take the tissue box and on the opposite side of the opening, draw around the end of the kitchen roll tube. Cut the hole out.

2 Decorate the box with tissue paper, making sure no light gets in. Tape the magnifying glass to the end of the kitchen roll tube and push the other end into the box.

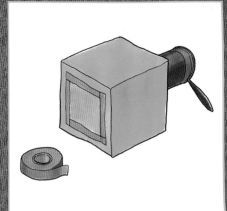

3 Cut a sheet of tracing paper and tape it to the opening of the box. It needs to be stretched very flat, with no creases.

4 Point the camera at a bright object and move the kitchen roll tube in and out until a sharp image appears on the tracing paper.

Wild-West cacti garden

With just a little bit of green-fingered magic and some imagination, you can recreate an **AMERICAN FRONTIER** in a mini garden. Just watch out for the **ARROWS**!

You will need

- Shallow pot
- Gravel
- Cactus potting mix
- Gloves
- Sand and toys

1 Put a layer of gravel into the shallow pot. Cover it with a 2.5cm (1in) layer of cactus potting mix, leaving holes for the cacti.

2 Add the cacti to the tray and push soil around their bases with a spoon. Be sure to wear thick gloves so you don't get prickled!

3 Cacti don't need a lot of water, which is how they survive in harsh desert environments. So, just lightly mist the soil every few days.

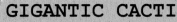

Attack!

GIGANTIC CACTI
Did you know that the giant Saguaro cactus found in Arizona, USA, can grow to be more than 20m (70ft) tall!

Decorate your
garden with sand
paths and toys to
give it that
wild-west feel

DIY crazy golf

Crazy golf is a great way to spend an afternoon but it's not something you can do whenever you want. Or is it? Well, with a little know-how, you can **PLAY A ROUND** in the comfort of your home.

Start off by hitting through a kitchen roll tube

Turn shoe boxes into obstacles or tunnels

Fill trays with water and sand. Don't hit the ball into them!

Use planks as ramps to make the holes even harder

HOW TO PLAY

1. Use bricks, wood, and cardboard to make some courses. Try to make each one different. Each course needs a hole and a starting point.

2. Try to get the ball in the hole in the fewest number of shots. The player with the lowest score wins.

A hole in 1, 2, 3

No golf course is complete without holes. So, our crazy golf course uses these little holes, whether you're indoors or out.

1 Cut out pieces of card in the shape of a triangle, and stick them to a wooden skewer or piece of bamboo with some tape.

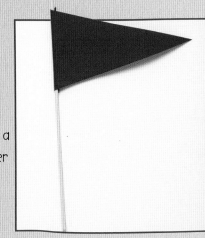

2 Wrap a can with anything you like: astroturf, wrapping paper, or even newspaper. Be careful of the sharp edges.

3 Stick your flag to the hole and put plasticine at the base to keep the can steady. Now, you're ready to tee-off!

Use a wrapping paper tube as a super-long tunnel

Planks of wood can become walls to bounce your shots off

Stack up bricks and try to weave the ball in between them

Put the hardest obstacle at the end of the course!

Make a board game

If you've had enough of Monopoly, Cluedo, and Snakes and Ladders, then perhaps it's time to **INVENT YOUR OWN GAME**. You don't need lots of equipment – just pens, card, dice, and, most importantly, people to play with.

Start

The first thing you need to think of is what your game is going to be about (a theme). It can be anything you like!

To make the board, divide a sheet of card into squares with a ruler. Decorate the board with drawings that match your theme.

Can't think of a theme for your game? How about an alien invasion?

In sequence fill the squares with numbers, from 1 to whatever the final square is.

Make counters out of card. Again, try to make them match your theme.

As a treat, give the winner a bar of chocolate!

GO BACK
3
SPACES

Give your game a trial run to make sure it worksssss

Fill the squares with rules such as "go forward two squares", or "miss a go". It's your game, so make up unusual rules.

MISS A TURN

Roll the dice. The winner is the first person to get to the final square!

Game over

Become a detective

Nobody has the same **FINGERPRINTS** as you – they are unique. This makes fingerprints incredibly useful for solving crimes. So, see if you can detect which of your friends has touched what.

You will need

- Inkpad
- Notebook or paper
- Cocoa powder
- Paintbrush
- Clear tape
- Pieces of card

1 Ask your "suspects" to put their fingers on the inkpad then press them into a notebook or paper. Note down whose prints are whose.

2 Send your friends into the kitchen and ask them each to touch just one thing. Now, seek out prints on doors, windows, and mugs.

3 Dip a paintbrush in the cocoa powder, shake off the excess, and apply powder to surfaces that you think might have prints on.

4 When you find a good print, apply a piece of tape and pull it off in one smooth motion. Stick it to a piece of card to preserve it.

5 Compare these prints with those you took earlier. Do you have some matching ones? Can you tell who touched what?

TOP TIP
Afterwards, make sure you clean up and wash your hands. Time for a mug of cocoa and detective movie?

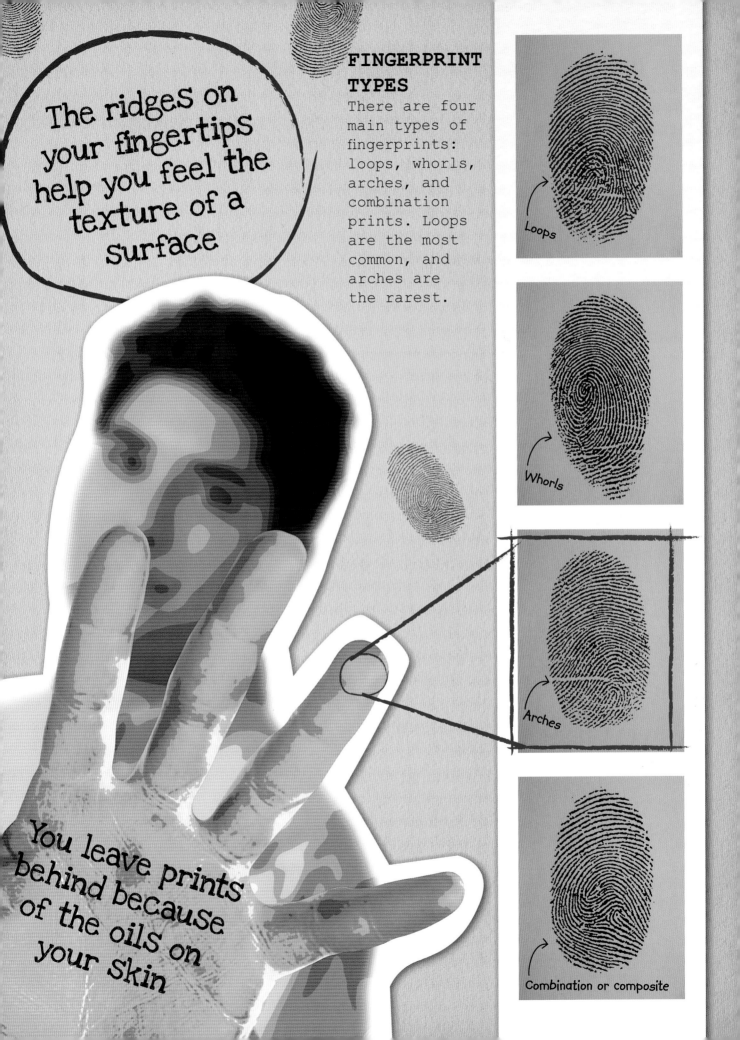

The ridges on your fingertips help you feel the texture of a surface

FINGERPRINT TYPES

There are four main types of fingerprints: loops, whorls, arches, and combination prints. Loops are the most common, and arches are the rarest.

Loops

Whorls

Arches

Combination or composite

You leave prints behind because of the oils on your skin

Magic tricks

Everybody should have a few tricks up their sleeve. If you want to become **A MASTER OF ILLUSION**, then start off with these two simple tricks.

Watch one coin become two

Convince your audience that you've transformed one coin into two before their very eyes, using a sleight of hand. If only!

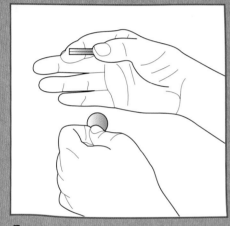

1 Place the two identical coins horizontally between your thumb and index finger. Hold the other coin in your other hand.

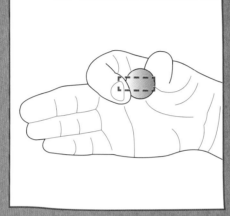

2 Place the smaller coin vertically between your thumb and index finger so it covers the large coins. This is the trick's starting point.

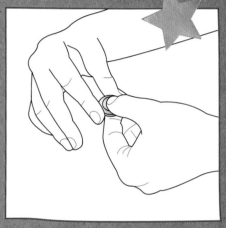

3 Show the small coin to the audience. Put your hands together and use your thumb to slide the smaller coin over the larger ones.

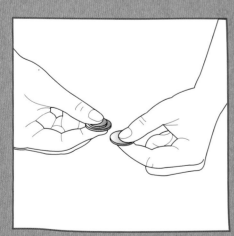

4 Quickly split the coins so that you hold a large coin in one hand, and a large coin with the small coin on top of it in the other hand.

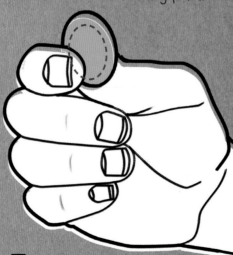

5 Turn your hands up to face the audience. Because the small coin was on top, it will be hidden, leaving just the large coins visible.

Perform the trick quickly so your audience never sees the hidden coin

Card psychic

Fool your friends into thinking they have any say in the matter of this card trick. With a little misdirection, you'll be in charge from step 1.

TOP TIP
Practise, practise, practise. You need to feel confident in how to perform a trick to be convincing.

1 Before you start, pick a card, such as the ace of hearts, and put it on top of the deck. Write it on a piece of paper and put it in your pocket.

2 Take the cards and push with your thumb the top four cards into your palm; the ace will be at the bottom. Hold the cards apart with a finger.

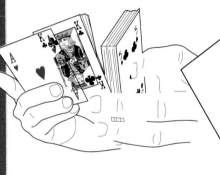

Ace of hearts

3 Spread the other cards on top and ask someone to point to one. Split the deck at this point, and slide the four hidden cards underneath.

4 Put the deck back together and reveal the bottom card to the audience. It'll be the card you put there, not the one pointed to.

5 Reach into your pocket and pull out the piece of paper. Show it to the audience – they'll think you have psychic powers!

MISDIRECTION
The secret to a good magic show is being confident and putting on a good show. If you're entertaining in your delivery, you can distract or misdirect the audience to pull off your trick.

If you want to be a **BALLOON WIZARD** then it's good to know that all that twisting and bending is **EASIER THAN IT LOOKS**. So, buy some special balloons and practise making these two simple ones to start with.

Make a Sword

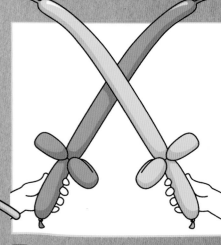

Be sure to use modelling balloons

You can twist in either direction

1 Blow up a balloon, leaving about 2.5cm (1in) at the end deflated. This extra air stops the balloon from bursting whenever you twist it.

2 Twist the balloon about 12cm (5in) from the knot. Twist it around a few times so that it doesn't unwind when you let go.

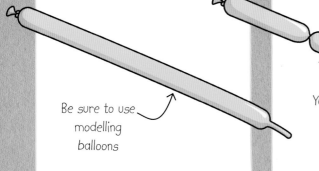
Bend about 7.5cm (3in) from the twist, then fold it into the first twist, making a loop

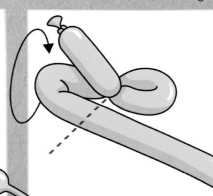

3 Bend the balloon towards the deflated end.

4 Another 7.5cm (3in) from the loop you just made, fold the balloon over and twist it in the same place to make a second loop.

5 Adjust the sword so that it's nice and straight, with the hilt in line with the blade. Time for a wibbly wobbly sword fight!

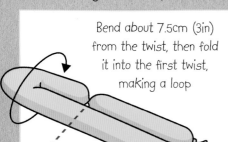

Grrr, take that!

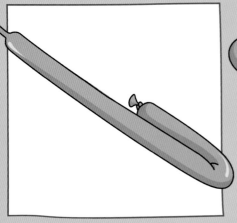

1 Inflate a balloon with about 10cm (4in) deflated. Make a fold about 20cm (8in) away from the knot.

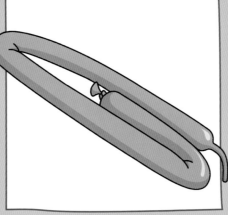

2 Fold the tail again so that the end lines up with the first fold. The balloon should look a bit like a paperclip.

3 Where all three bits meet – by the knot – twist together. You should have two loops and a tube sticking up, as shown.

Create a Swan

4 Pull one of the loops up through the other one to make the body. The long tube will be the neck and head.

5 Fold the neck down away from the body as shown. Hold the neck tightly, bend, and squeeze it. Let go and it should stay in place.

Secret spy gear

Want to be the next **JAMES BOND**? Collect great **GADGETS**? Be a master of **DISGUISE**? Here's the basics you'll need for any **SPY IN TRAINING**.

You will need

- Baking soda
- Water
- A bowl
- A cotton bud
- Recycled paper

A NEWSPAPER PROP

When you're shadowing a target you sometimes need to hide in plain sight. By cutting some eyeholes out of a newspaper you can watch your target without them seeing you.

DISGUISES

When a spy's cover is blown his mission is usually over. That's why a spy has to become a master of disguise. Experiment with ways to slip by undetected or to create new aliases. Here are some suggestions:

Hats
Moustaches
Glasses
Wigs

BLENDING IN

A disguise should help you blend in, not stand out. So anything that looks over the top will only make you look suspicious!

TOP TIP

For more spy gear, don't forget the periscope (pages 6–7) and secret book safe (pages 16–17).

Invisible ink

Relay a secret message to a friend using this invisible ink. We use a picture to give you the general idea.

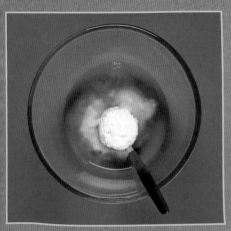  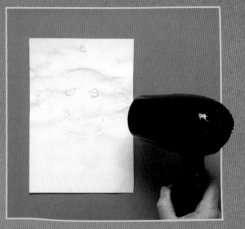

1 Put equal parts of baking soda and water into a bowl and stir together. You don't need much, and the baking soda won't fully dissolve, but that doesn't matter.

2 Dip the cotton bud into the mixture and use it to write on the paper. Let the paper dry and slip it to your accomplice (look out for people over your shoulder).

3 The reader has to hold a hairdryer near to the paper to reveal the hidden message!

The heat of the hairdryer reacts with the baking soda and spells out your message

Flipbook animation

Bring your **DRAWINGS TO LIFE**. A flipbook animation is a series of pictures that change a little bit each time, so that it **LOOKS LIKE IT MOVES** if you flick through them! Tell a little cartoon story, such as a fish eating another fish.

1 Decide on what you want to animate. It can be anything you want, but keep it simple at first. Start on the back page and lightly sketch your first drawing.

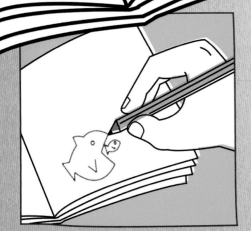

2 Working backwards, sketch the other stages. It might seem strange, but it means that you can trace parts that look the same.

3 Every few pages, flip the pages to check that your animation looks okay. Fix any problems with your eraser.

4 When you're happy with it, go over the lines in bold and add colour. Thumb through the pages and see the animation in all its glory!

Have a doodle
to come up
with ideas!

STOP MOTION

Your animation can be based on photos too. For example, take a photograph of a glass of water. Take a sip without moving it, then take another photo, and repeat. Combine the pictures using software on a computer. You'll see the water vanish.

ANIMATION IDEAS

If you can't think of what to draw, copy the sequence below. Once you've got the hang of it, you can try a bouncing ball or a moving stick man. It's up to you!

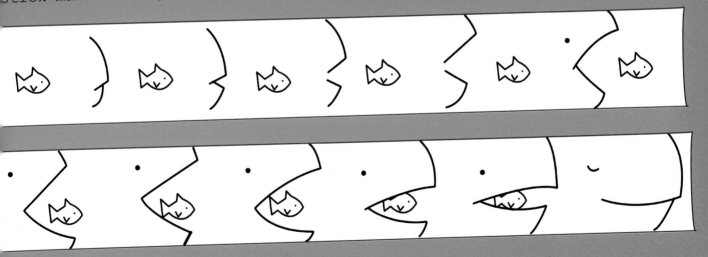

Write a scary story

There's no need to save all the scaring for Halloween. Whether you want to amass your own set of scary stories or invite friends over for a **SCARY STORYTELLING SESSION**, here's the basics for any young writer in training.

PICK A THEME
The best writers draw ideas from real life. Try to think of what scares you and make it a part of your story. Whether it's ghosts, aliens, monsters, or something else – it'll be easier for you to imagine what your characters will feel like if you think like they would!

Structure
Every good story needs a beginning, middle, and an end.

Don't concentrate on anything specific at this point, it's just to help you later.

Before you start, sketch up a quick outline or map of how your story might end and begin, and then think of ways to connect the two.

BUILD TENSION
Suspense – or not knowing what's going to happen – is what makes a story scary. Try to keep the audience on their toes by not making it obvious what's going to happen next.

SCENE SETTING

To make your story believable, it needs to feel like it takes place somewhere real. It all depends on what your theme is. If you really want to make your story scary, have it take place somewhere your friends know, that will make it easier for them to imagine it being real!

Hero

Your story needs a character for people to identify with. It's up to you what kind of person they can be: male, female, strong, weak, scared, fearless. Sometimes the best characters are flawed. Think of what your character would be thinking or feeling and work it into the story.

Villain

Every story needs a convincing villain, and the best ones are the ones that are equal but opposite to the hero. They can be supernatural, a person, a monster — it's up to you. Just be sure to focus on the villain as much as the hero.

AND TO FINISH

The ending is usually what the audience will remember most, so make it memorable. You can have a happy ending, a funny one to break the tension, or a "twist", where something totally unexpected happens. The most important part of the ending is always to leave the reader wanting more. Time for a sequel?

Let's have a water fight!

When the temperature's rising what could be better than a team game mixed with a **WATER FIGHT**? This game – **CAPTURE THE FLAG** – requires speed, accuracy, teamwork, and tactics. So, who will **WIN** and who will get the **WETTEST**?

How to play

Fill up water balloons and split into two teams. Place a different coloured flag at two bases at opposite ends of a field or park.

The object of the game is to capture the other team's flag and take it back to your base. In order to score, **BOTH** flags have to be at your base.

TACTIC #1

Teamwork is important. Each team needs a captain, who'll then give each player a job to do – attack or defence. If everybody tried to capture the flag, there wouldn't be anybody left to defend their own!

RULES

• **WATER BALLOONS ONLY**, water guns are too easy to hit people with!

• If you get hit, you have to leave the field for a **30-SECOND TIME-OUT** before you are allowed to re-enter the game.

• If you're hit while carrying a flag, drop it on the floor where you are. Either team can then pick it up to capture it or return it to base.

• The first team to **THREE CAPTURES** wins.

TACTIC #3

Try to coordinate attacks to knock out several of the other team at once, so they're on time-out at the same time. Then there won't be many left to defend their base and flag.

TACTIC #2

Pay attention to ammo supplies. Don't waste your ammo on long throws, try to get in close. Also, check out the other team's ammo levels – when they're low that's the perfect time to attack!

During the festival of Songkran, people all over Thailand have a giant water fight in the streets!

AHOY THERE! Pirates live a life of adventure on the high seas, and so can you! Search for the **BURIED TREASURE** and **DO BATTLE** against your fellow pirates with these fab props.

You will need

- Two pieces of cardboard
- Glue
- Black tape
- Tin foil

Cardboard cutlass

The cutlass is the weapon of choice of pirates everywhere. So if you plan on sailing the seven seas, you'll need one of your own.

1 Mark out the cutlass shape on two pieces of cardboard as shown. Cut them out and glue them together.

2 Once the glue has dried, wrap black tape around the hilt, and foil around the blade.

Treasure map

Any pirate worth his salt is always looking to bag some booty. Here's a fun way of making your own treasure map. If you want, you can make a map of your house or garden and hide something for your friends to find.

1 Tear around the edges of a piece of paper. Crumple it into a ball, then flatten it out, and lie it on old newspaper or card.

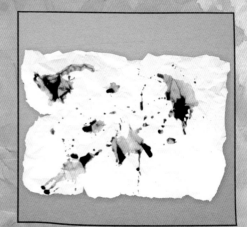

2 Put a few spoonfuls of the tea or coffee onto the paper and rub it in with your hands. Try to cover the whole page.

3 Wait for five minutes and get an adult to dry it with the hairdryer. Make sure that they don't hold the hairdryer too close to the page.

4 Once it's dried and looks old, use the markers to draw landmarks on your map. Show rocks, jungles, caves, and don't forget X marks the spot!

Olympics outdoors

The **OLYMPIC GAMES** may only come around every four years, but if you host your own, you can go for gold whenever you want!

INVITE YOUR FRIENDS over and make a list of events you want to compete in. It's up to you to decide which ones, but try to have at least five. Here are a few suggestions:

Bean bag shot putt

Obstacle course

Standing long jump

Hoop toss

Relay race

Three-legged race

Flying discus

MAKING MEDALS

You can't have an Olympics without medals. Before you start, work out how many events you're going to have, and make three medals (gold, silver, and bronze) for each one.

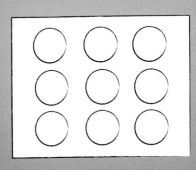

1 Use the can as a guide on the card to draw around to make circles. Draw enough for all your upcoming Olympic events.

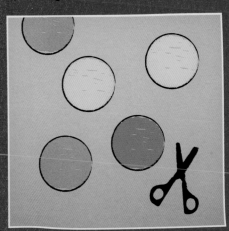

2 Cut the circles out and either paint or colour them in with markers. Make one-third of them gold or yellow, one-third silver or grey, and the last third brown.

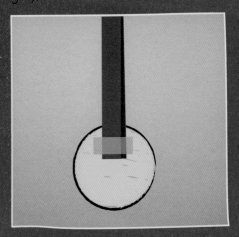

3 Cut the ribbon into lengths that are long enough to hang around your neck. Tape them to the back of the card to finish the medals.

Egg and spoon race

Bin basketball

Sack race

ON THE PODIUM

Once the events are over, award the winners their medals on a podium. Make one from anything strong enough to support your weight, such as crates or wooden boxes.

(59)

Cowboy capers

Make like a cowboy in the Wild West and learn **HOW TO MAKE AND USE A LASSO**. You might not have herds of cattle to round up or need to lasso and bring down calves to brand, but it **FEELS GREAT** to try – practise on **A CHAIR**. Cowboy hat optional, but yee-haws essential.

You will need

- Rope
- Chair
- Cowboy hat (optional)

Yee-haw Cowboy!

1 After making your lasso, hold the rope coil in one hand. Make a noose 60cm (24in) across, and hold it above the knot, in your other hand.

2 Hold your lasso to the side and spin it around in a clockwise motion. Relax your wrist so that it rotates nice and smoothly.

3 While still rotating the lasso, lift it over your head. Swing the rope as if you were spinning a hoop around your wrist.

Tie a lariat knot

Here's how to tie the special knot – a lariat – to make a lasso work.

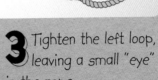

Howdy partner!

Tie a knot here to keep the lariat's shape

Feed this end through the loop to finish

1 Make a loose loop in a length of rope. Slip the end of the rope through it.

2 Pull the end of the rope back up through the loop, as shown.

3 Tighten the left loop, leaving a small "eye" in the rope.

4 Pull the knot tight. Then feed the long end of rope through the eye.

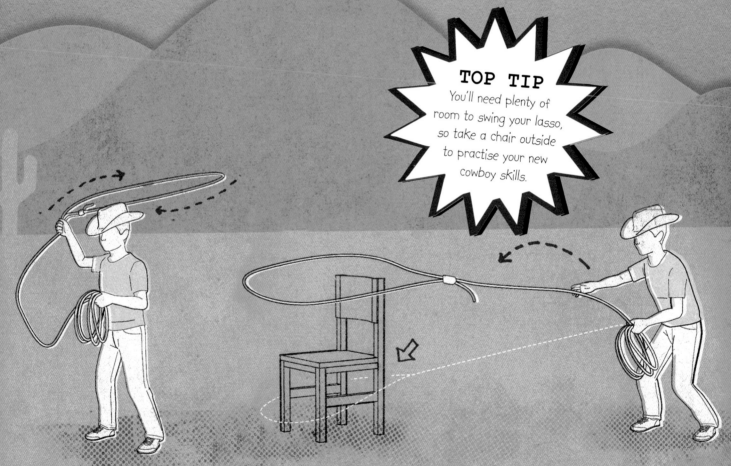

TOP TIP
You'll need plenty of room to swing your lasso, so take a chair outside to practise your new cowboy skills.

4 Aim at the chair and bring your hand forward. Let go of the noose. It should shoot forward in front of you.

5 If your aim is spot on, the noose should wrap around the chair. Pull the rope tight to tighten the noose around it. Yee-hah!

That's impossible!

Jaws will be **DROPPING OPEN** in amazement when you show friends and family any of these **UNBELIEVABLE TRICKS**. Afterwards, you can show them how it works or keep it secret.

Egg in a bottle

Ask your friends if they can think of a way to get a boiled egg into a bottle without breaking it. After they've given up trying, show them how it's done.

1 Boil and peel an egg and place it on the rim of the bottle. Show your friends that there's no way the egg will fit through.

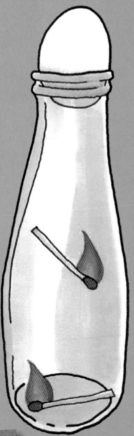

2 Ask an adult to light two matches and drop them into the bottle. Quickly place the egg on the rim.

Air presses on the egg from outside

TOP TIP
You might need to try out a few glass bottle shapes to see which fits an egg best.

3 After a few seconds the egg will squeeze through the bottle neck into the bottom of the bottle.

HOW IT WORKS
When the matches go out, the warm air inside the bottle cools and the pressure drops. The air pressure outside the bottle is now higher, so the air tries to push its way in, taking the egg with it.

Gravity-defying forks

With some precise positioning, you can balance things n ways that seem impossible. It's all about controlling n object's centre of gravity, which is the point at which its weight is spread.

1 Take two forks and link the prongs together. This can be quite fiddly, so you might want to do this before you start the trick.

2 Push a toothpick through the middle of the prongs. Then balance the toothpick on the rim of a glass.

3 Once it's balanced, ask an adult to light a match and set light to the toothpick on the inside of the glass. It'll burn away, leaving the forks balancing on almost nothing!

⚠️

Book friction

Take two equally sized books and interlace the pages so they overlap each other by about 5cm (2in). Give the books to a friend and ask them to try to pull them apart. It's almost impossible!

TOP TIP
The more pages that overlap, the better the trick will work. Spend a bit of time interlacing the pages.

Index

A
alien
    as a theme 40–41, 52
    masks 14–15
animation 50–51

B
balancing forks 63
balloon
    drag racer 8–9
    shapes 46–47
    water 54–55
board game, making 40–41
bongos 21
book safe 16–17
bottle
    car 8–9
    fountain 28–29
    rocket 32–33

C
cacti 36–37
camera, pinhole 34–35
camouflage 7
capture the flag 54–55
card trick 45
carton 6–7, 14–15
chocolate 41
coin trick 44
cornflour 30
cowboys 36–37, 60–61
crazy golf 38–39
cutlass 56

D
deck of cards 44
detective 42–43
disguise 48
drums 21

E
egg in a bottle 62

F
fingerprint
    making 42–43
    types 43
fizzy drink fountain 28–29
flipbook animation 50–51

G
games
    board 40–41
glow-in-the-dark jelly 22–23
golf 38–39
guitar, playing 20

H
hairdryer 49, 57
halloween 14, 22
hero 53

I J
ink 42
invisible ink 49
jars 20
jelly, glow-in-the-dark 22–23

K L
knight puppet 18–19
lassoing a chair 60–61
light
    reflected 7
    ultraviolet 22–23

M
magnets 12
magnifying glass 34–35
medals 59
microwave 22, 26–27
milk
    carton masks 14–15

mints 28
mirror 6–7
molecules 26
monster
    made of soap 26–27
music
    instruments 20–21

O P
Olympics 58–59
paper 10, 42
    cups 18–19
    fasteners 14
    planes 10–11
    tissue 34–35
    tracing 34–35
papier mâché 24–25
periscope 6–7
pirates 56–57
pressure 25, 32–33
pump 32–33
puppet 18–19

Q R
quinine 22–23
recycling 12–13, 48
robots 12–13, 34
rocket
    car 8–9
rubbish 12, 18–19, 38–39

S
scary story 52–53
secret
    agent 6, 48–49
    book safe 16–17
    spy gear 48–49
slime 30–31
soap
    monsters 26–27
songkran 55
story
    animated 50
    scary 52–53
submarine 6

T
tonic water 22–23
tricks
    impossible 62–63
    magic 44–45

V
villain 53
volcano 24–25

W
water fight 54–55
wild-west 36–37

X, Y
xylophone 20

PICTURE CREDITS
The publisher would like to thank the following for their kind permission to reproduce their photographs:

(Key: a-above; b-below/bottom; c-centre; f-far; l-left; r-right; t-top)

40 Dorling Kindersley: Gary Kings - modelmaker (c). 41 Dorling Kindersley: Graham High at Centaur Studios - modelmaker (cr); Thomas Marent (cl); Gary Kings - modelmaker (bc).

All other images © Dorling Kindersley For further information see: www.dkimages.com

DK WOULD LIKE TO THANK
Nikki Simms for proofreading, George Nimmo for production assistance, Sonia Charbonnier for technical assistance, and Romaine Werblow for image sourcing.